S0-BCG-104

Jack Pollard's

COMPLETE GUIDE TO

AUSTRALIAN

FISHING

This edition Published and distributed by
The Book Company International Pty Ltd
9/9-13 Winbourne Road
Brookvale 2100, Sydney NSW Australia

Copyright © 1995

Publisher: Glenn Johnstone
Production Team: Leslie Krey, Gillian Blackman, Russell Perry

Cover photography and design by Robyn Latimer
Typeset by Robyn Latimer
Produced by Mandarin Offset.

The publisher would like to acknowledge
Harbord Tackle Supply
16c Lawrence Street, Harbord NSW 2096
for supplying props for the cover photography.

The views and opinions contained in this work are the authors
and not the publishers. The publisher does not accept responsibility
for any inaccuracy or incorrect or untrue information or facts.

Jack Pollard's
COMPLETE GUIDE TO

AUSTRALIAN
FISHING

INTRODUCTION

The purpose of this book is to take beginners through the basics of successful fishing and to allow oldhands to brush up on their techniques and knowledge of our most popular fish species.

Over the last few years a lot of talented biologists have joined in research work in our museums and fisheries departments and some very intriguing new material has been unearthed on all the best known fishes. Even oldhands who have spent their lives fishing for sport can benefit from the results of all this research. The fish don't change, of course, but our information on them needs constant up-dating. Fishing tackle has certainly improved dramatically and the benefits to all sports fishermen from this are also discussed in this work. Recreational fishing has always been an important part of the Australian way of life and the standard of information available to amateurs these days has never been so diverse and expertly based.

contents

ACKNOWLEDGEMENTS

The full colour illustrations of popular Australian fish in this book were painted by Walter Stackpool. The photographs in the book came from the Australian Picture Library or the Jack Pollard Collection.
The material in this book on recommended rigs is based on the work of veteran fishing writer Dick Lewers.

CHAPTER ONE

Tackle That Does the Job

Before you go out on your first fishing outing, give some thought to the type of water you intend to fish and the species you are likely to find there. Bait shops, marine staff and the fishing columns of local newspapers will identify the species and a few minutes discussion in the tackle shop of your choice will confirm the fish that are being caught in the region and the basic tackle required.

Resist efforts to load you up with costly rods, reels and fancy lures. Make your initial purchases simple. A lot of very good fish are caught on lines that wind round a piece of cork or a plastic spool winder. Handlines are a practical inexpensive way to start and there are a few basics you need to understand before you open the purse strings.

Firstly, you must appreciate that metrication has had less acceptance in fishing than any other sport. The average angler still measures the breaking strain of lines in the imperial measure, pounds, and ignores or is completely unaware of the term "newton" to describe the line strength. Tackle shops may try to comply with the law by attaching stickers converting line breaking strengths to newtons, but the stickers are quickly discarded. Amateur fishing records are judged in kilograms and the select few who apply for records express the breaking strain of the lines they used in kilograms, but the average angler, interested only in catching fish for an appetising meal, still talks in pounds.

Secondly, you need to consider the habits and the physical makeup of the fish you are seeking. if you intend to join the hordes of anglers who fish for sand whiting in the Iluka-Yamba district or at places like Tweed Heads or Maroochydore, you will only need light tackle and baits like peeled prawns, yabbies, tiny crabs or live worms, plus small hooks and a light sinker. But if you want to go out into the surf for your whiting you will need a stronger line and heavier sinker.

Sand whiting are voracious feeders, but they don't cut through lines like Australian salmon which bite in fumbling style and become quite acrobatic when hooked. Tailor on the other hand have a vicious bite despite their small mouths and need to be played firmly without tearing the mouth. Nannygai will try to twist the line when hooked by swimming in circles and must be firmly drawn in once they are hooked. Snapper in their mature stage can crush or break weak hooks in their hard, bony mouths.

From these few examples the novice angler will see the need to study the quarry. This is one of the satisfying benefits of sport fishing, the realisation that a knowledge of Australia's fish behaviour brings better catches. You need to think like a fish to catch one.

Successful fishermen begin their outings in the kitchen or in their workshops. They study hook sizes and shapes, practise the essential knots, clean their gear, and make sure their lines are clear of knots and tangles. Some even make moulds in which they melt down their personal sinkers. Others have covers knitted for their reels by kindly grandparents or mothers.

After a few outings with handlines, many casual anglers will appreciate the importance of learning a few basic knots. The nylon they use is a modern invention which, unlike the cord lines they replaced, is tricky to tie, and can be tied in hundreds of ways. It is wise when you begin to learn the tricks of sport fishing that you concentrate on your fundamental skills, such as knotting a hook to a line, mending a broken line, and knotting the end of your line to your spool or reel. Specialist knots can come later. Learn a few you can tie in the dark at the start.

THE BLOOD KNOT:

This knot is unchallenged as the one to use in securely joining a broken line. The experts recommend that four turns on each side for a line with a breaking strain below 6kg and three turns for lines heavier than that. Always remember, however, that even

the best knots weaken the line they are intended to repair. Procedures for tying the basic knots is shown in the accompanying diagrams and are worth careful study.

Once you have become accustomed to handling nylon lines and are aware of the fact that some brands are softer than others and prone to poor knot strength, you can consider the hook you intend to tie on the end of it. Hooks today are machine cut and come from tackle shops with sharp points but are not needle-sharp. Thus it is wise to increase the sharpness of whatever size you select with a file or stone so that the hook will more easily snag on the bony mouths.

Never use a rusty, badly blunted or misshapen hook. There is no need to because hooks are probably the cheapest part of a fisherman's gear. Match the hook you pick to the line. Big hooks are ineffective on small lines, and you must use hooks that can handle the bait of your choice. It makes no sense to attach a big hook to a weak line. In selecting a hook, try to pick one that is best for the species you are seeking and the conditions in which you fish. Fish with hard bony mouths require a firm, sharp hook with a barb not too far back from the point. Fishing for bream, using soft bait such as pipi, you will do best with a short-shanked, thin-wire sneck hook. For tailor, which have big, soft mouths

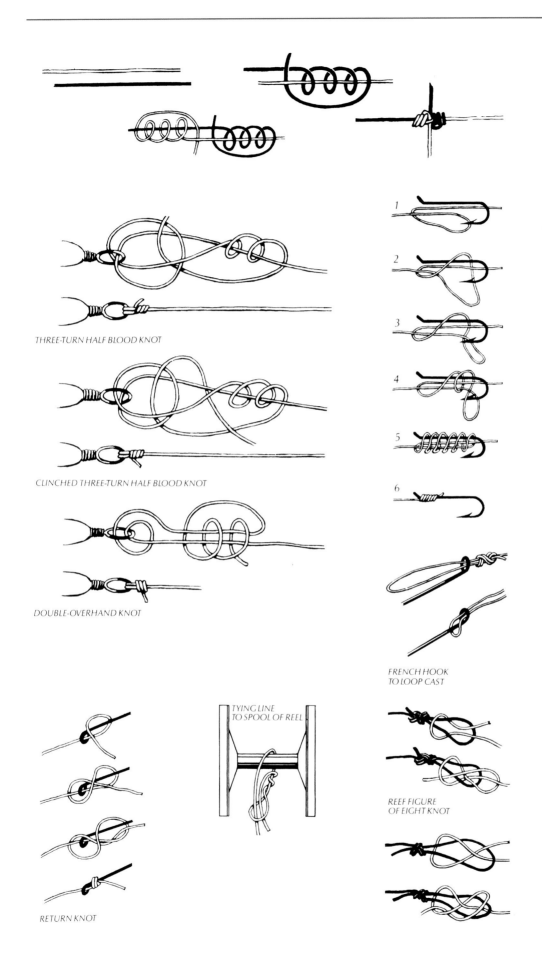

THREE-TURN HALF BLOOD KNOT

CLINCHED THREE-TURN HALF BLOOD KNOT

DOUBLE-OVERHAND KNOT

1

2

3

4

5

6

FRENCH HOOK
TO LOOP CAST

TYING LINE
TO SPOOL OF REEL

REEF FIGURE
OF EIGHT KNOT

RETURN KNOT

*Recommended
swivels and clips*

BARREL

BOX

THREE-WAY BARREL

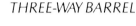

SNAP

TORPEDO

THREE-WAY BOX

STUB

HEAVY GAMEFISH

and slash at the bait, a long-shanked hook with a wide gape and the barb set well back from the point is best.

Hooks come in a bewildering range of forms and a few minutes in a tackle shop will show you that they have

inspired a jargon on their own. They may seem a small item but large companies devote their entire production effort to producing them, and from the flood of hooks that come into Australia and New Zealand a range of distinctive patterns and favoured types have emerged.

The most popular are Kendall Kirb of Kirby, a general purpose hook with a round bow which slides the point of draw to the front; French, a strong rigid hook favoured for fish with bony mouths or for very tough baits; Viking, a lighter, high quality forged hook with reversed turned-down ball eye; Suicide, a short shanked rounded hook of strength and rigidity which works well with soft bait; Beak, a modified form of Suicide with a rounded bend, slightly longer and more rigid shank; Sneck, a short-shanked hook with a very square bow, short spear and the barb set fairly close to the point; Carlisle, along-shanked hook ideal for chaining several together; Limerick, a strong, heavy-gauge straight hook without kirb, with a long, straight spear that is difficult for fish to throw; O'Shaughnessy, a high grade forged hook similar in pattern to the Limerick in which great care has been taken with pointing and tempering; Swordfish, a high grade forged and eyed hook ideal for tuna, marlin and medium-weight game fish; Sea Master, an extra-strong, high grade forged hook with a knife-edge point and a brazed, tapered ring eye.

SINKERS AND SWIVELS:

The beginner often makes his worst mistake in his choice of sinker, invariably attaching a sinker of shape and size that is a handicap rather than an assistance. They usually err by picking sinkers that are needlessly heavy under the misapprehension that it will help them get their line out further when they cast. The wise angler selects sinkers judiciously, aware that they are not merely attached to a line to keep the hook and bait below the surface. Sinkers vary a low from State to State or even from one location to another only a few kilometres away and it pays when venturing into new territory to study what the locals are using.

Common Australian sinkers are: Bean of Barrel sinkers, a running sinker for estuaries usually used with half a match to position them where they are required; Running Shot or Split Shot, small spherical sinkers with holes in the centre split into halves that are pinched on to lines; Snapper Lead, the most favoured type for use in deep sea fishing or when fishing over reefs, popular among anglers wanting more distance in their casts; Channel of Pickers Doom, a running sinker preferred to strong currents or running tides; Beach or Bar, a circular sinker usually with small bumpers for use in light surfs or over sand; Helmet, a heavier sinker that is ideal for casting in rough water that can hold a bait in a feeding area.

Stainless steel split rings which come in a variety of types are used for attaching lures to hooks, but brass rings are recommended in some rigs. Simple barrel swivels are used as stoppers on running rigs. Ball bearing snap swivels are used for trolling and barrel types for cast. The secret is to use swivels for what they are intended - to reduce line twist, remembering that the swivel must be equal to the line strain being used. Slim swivels suit light lines. Don't make the mistake of thinking you only have to put a swivel on to prevent your line twisting. Swivels will reduce twist but seldom eliminate it entirely.

RODS AND REELS:

Australians fishing in saltwater favour the sidecast reel, the centrepin reel, the threadline or fixed spool reel, the push-button or closed face reel, and the bait-casting reel. Trout fisherman use reels with far smaller line capacity, light enough to balance properly with graphite, boron and kelvar, some of which are made from magnesium and carbon fibre. All of the above reels have their advantages but the two most popular reels outside of Queensland

Typical sportfishing reels:

Top right, *Daiwa casting reel;*
Top left, *Roddy spinning reel;*

Centre, *Galion fixed spool reel, (right) and the Intrepid fixed spool reel;*

Bottom, *the Roddy spinning reel, (left), and the Daiwa spinning reel.*

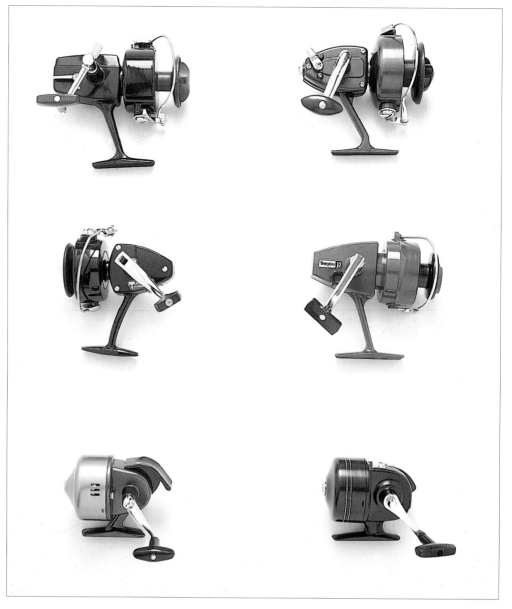

are the threadline reel and the closed face reel. In Queensland sidecast reels from the Alvey company dominate all forms of beach, estuary and reef fishing.

The threadline reel, which is always mounted under the rod, is the best for novices because it performs several complicated tasks simply by turning the handle which is attached to the body. This rotates a main gear mesh with a pinion gear, a cuplike fitting that envelopes the spool and

revolves around it. The rotating head revolves, carrying the line and pick-up assembly with it, trapping the line and winding it round the spool, automatically cross-laying the line on the spool. The vital cross-laying is achieved simply and easily by the threadline mechanism.

The closed face reel is fitted on top of the rod and many consider it easier to use than the threadline reel. The spool and the mechanism are fully enclosed, apart from the small circular hole in the centre of the cone covering the spool, through which the line passes. By using a pistol grip, the push button on the closed face reel drops to a convenient height for the thumb. When the thumb button is held down, pins on the pick-up head trap the line against the lip of the winding cup until the fisherman releases it. After completing the cast, the angler simply turns the handle to re-engage or extend the pick-up pins, which then trap and hold the line.

Centrepin are the simplest of all the reels, comprising a spool carrying the line revolving on a ball bearing or bushes attached to a bolt mounted to a backing plate. They are usually direct drive without gears, sometimes with basic drag systems. The centrepin reel has largely disappeared except among luderick fishermen who find it ideal for bringing in fish against the rise and fall of the sea. With the centrepin it is easy to let the fish run and then wind up again rapidly. With a thumb on the spool the centrepin answers quickly, whereas a threadline reel could not cope with this situation.

The sidecast reel has become a feature of Australian east coast angling. They are basically centrepin reels that can be twisted or rotated through 90 degrees. They are particularly effective in casting, with the line flowing out in the manner of a fixed spool reel over the lip of the spool. When the cast is completed, the spool is twisted back to regain alignment with the rod. The sidecast combines the best qualities of the centrepin with the easy casting performance of spinning reels, and has the advantage of being easy to maintain. Sidecast reels are ideal for hauling fish up cliff faces or on to high walls and jetties.

ROD SELECTION:

Before you buy a fishing rod, give some thought to where and how you intend to use it, the conditions in which you will fish, and the likely size of the fish you will catch. For the choice of rod is wide because of dramatic scientific changes over the last 40 years. Bamboo and cane rods still enthral oldtimers but the overwhelming majority of the rods used today are graphite, hollow fibreglass or materials such as kelvar or boron. Baitcast rods to carry sizeable baits and lures usually are between 1.5 and 2 metres in length, which for snapper and jewfish have slightly heavier tips and behave well during casts. Sidecast rods are between 3.5 to 4.5 metres long, with the real attached very close to the butt and will perform well on a variety of fish. If you are seeking big fish that require large baits, you will need a fast, tapered rod.

Don't be bewildered by tackle dealers' talk about the action of rods.

Surf fishermen enjoying casting with their sidecast reels in a rising surf. These reels have virtually taken over beach angling on the Australian east coast.

This is simply the qualities that permit a rod to recover from a bend, and the leverage you need when a fish starts lunging about when hooked. There are three basic actions for a rod, fast, medium and slow, and these depend on the length of the rod blank, and the number of wraps the manufacturers make around the steel mandrel when the blank is baked in an oven. Fast action rods are the type that flex along the top, with a "tippy" style motion.

Spinning rods are between 1.6 and 2.5 metres long with light tips for casting small baits, and a mid-section that stiffens into the butt. Fitted with a threadline reel, they suit fish up to 7kg, are simple to use, and can haul in fish of reasonable weight. They invariably have good drag action and

fast retrieve. Today's ultra-light spinning rods are remarkably strong and are ideal for single-handed casting and will stand up to prolonged fish fighting. Cork handles are recommended by experts as they transmit the feel of a fish's delicate nibbling.

Flyrods usually are sold in two pieces and are between 2.5 and 2.8 metres long, delivering the line smoothly with a small bend or load. Most are cork-handled and fitted with simple centrepin fly reels. In contrast, game-fishing rods have butts designed to play big, powerful fish and carry overhead reels with immense line capacity.

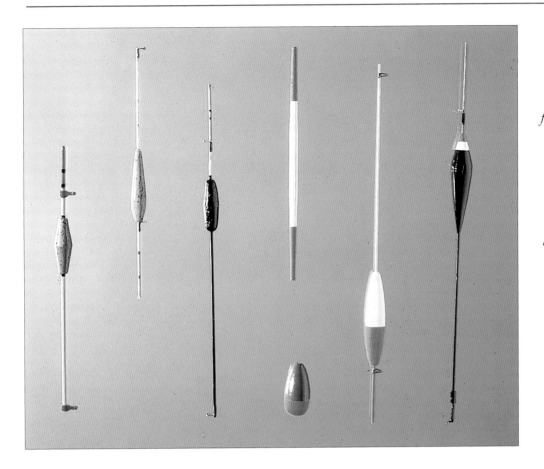

*Popular floats:
(L to R): A light
balsa and cork
float, a light cork
and cane runner
float, a cedar pencil,
an all purpose cork
and cane float, a
light cork and
metal float,
and a slim metal
and cane float;
below a Bobby cork.*

FLOATS AND NETS:

The basic purpose of a fishing float is to present the bait or lure to fish at the depths where the fish feed. The float chosen should support the bait and rig in use and give a quick indication of a bite. Given these simple aims, the angler is confronted by a bewildering array of floats, some ingenious, others worthless. Most anglers have more floats than they will ever use, which prompted one cynic to comment that floats catch more anglers than fish.

Luderick or blackfish fishermen need floats of very low buoyancy, such as a quill or pencil float. They can be used as fixed or running floats and are also handy for bream, garfish or in bait fishing for yellowtail. Bobby corks are preferred for estuary fishing when drifting baits from the shore for flathead. They are very effective with live baits. In rough conditions and strong winds when there is need to cast for a distance, heavier cork floats, usually with brass centre tubing, are preferred. Balloon and plastic bottle floats are used by game fishermen to get baits well down to tuna, kingfish or even sharks.

Fishing nets are very useful for fish that are too small to gaff and come in two main shapes - round nets for use in open water, and triangular, flat-fronted nets that can get down to the bottom in shallow water. Gaffs are barbless hooks that are driven into the fish to land it. They are sometimes fitted with detachable heads which can be released from the handle if a game fish makes an unexpected plunge.

CHAPTER TWO

Baits

and

Lures

First-rate freshwater bait: a bucket of freshly caught crayfish, known to Americans as freshwater shrimps.

All the popular species of fish are hunters who prefer their food alive. They will take dead bait and are regularly taken on fish fillets, crab meat, pieces of squid, octopi, pipis, cuttlefish, bread, dough, worm pieces, green weed, chicken gut, liver and pudding mixtures, but it is important to remember that their priority is for fresh food. They much prefer a live worm to a dead one, or a live, wriggling prawn to one that stinks from lying too long in a boat.

Preparing for a fishing outing, work out a way of keeping your bait as fresh as possible by storing it in a plastic ice bucket or some portable container that won't make it soft and soggy. Deep-freeze baits quickly deteriorate after thawing and prawns, pilchards and squid that may have been cheap in the markets often becomes useless as bait. If you plan to use fish fillets, make sure you salt them without delay. Salt has the effect of hardening the fillets and stops them shredding. If you only need to keep bait fresh for a day, a few ice cubes will probably do the trick.

Some bait fish, such as salmon or mullet, have large scales and need to be scaled before filleting. This allows salt to penetrate the skin and makes the cut baits far easier to handle. One of the best baits, blue mackerel, also known as common or greasy mackerel, softens rapidly after capture and has to be used immediately it is caught. Blue mackerel secured from a fish shop in reasonable condition requires salting to harden it up and then it will keep for several days, particularly if it is stored in absorbent wrapping such as newspaper. Bonito, another splendid bait, deteriorates quickly after death but keeps well if it is salted as soon as you get it home. Some shops, in fact, sell bonito fillets already salted.

Yellowtail or scad also soften rapidly, but the smaller fish make very good baits for use as whole fish. They too harden up if salted. Garfish are always a problem in hot weather and are usually not much

use unless they are used immediately after they are caught. They deteriorate faster than all other bait fish with their gut turning brown unless they are gutted and salted. Fresh mullet is an outstanding bait, but the quality appears to vary from State to State. Sale of mullet under a legal size is banned in southern States, but forms a large part of the bait sold in Queensland, where small whole mullet are classed as excellent bait for the larger reef fish. Salmon, or as the New Zealanders call it "kahawa" is an ideal bait for jewfish, tailor and bream and will stand up to storage as salted fillets.

The flesh of tommy ruff or herring is relished by the hungry fish species found in South Australia and Western Australia. In Queensland small pilchards or sardines are often used but they soften very quickly and need to be bound on to the hook, Silver trevally and northern school whiting usually turn up in the baits used by Queensland tourist charter boats.

Right round Australia, however, frozen prawns remain the most popular of all baits, and every year thousands of packets are sold from harbour, beach and estuary bait shops, garages, marinas and grocery shops. Most school kids start their fishing education using frozen prawns, though it is often not the best available bait, and quickly becomes useless in the sun. Make sure your prawns are fresh, but forget

Popular Bait Fish:
Common or Blue
Mackerel,
Pilchard, Bonito,
Sea Garfish.

them if you intend fishing in the surf or anywhere that turbulent waters might wash them from the hook. If you need to keep them for any length of time, remove the heads and pack the tails in sawdust or bran, placing them in a plastic bag for storage in an ice box

A more successful bait often overlooked by anglers unaware of how to handle them are the wide variety of

*Common Mackerel,
Pneumatophorus
australasicus.*

*Pilchard, Sardinops
neopilchardus*

worms easily found on our beaches. Beachworms occur in millions on the beaches of eastern Australia, and are highly valued by fishermen because of their great length and muscular bodies. They can be easily collected with a technique which in itself is fun. Simply insert a piece of decaying or bloody meat into a plastic bag or attach it to a piece of string. Then drag it along the sand in the shallow back-wash of the waves. The worms will poke their heads out of the sand in response to the smell of the meat, and as they break the low water surface can be easily spotted by an arrow-like ripple. Wait for the next wave because the worm will not emerge on a dry beach, positioning yourself where the worm was, and as it reappears lure it a little further out with the decaying meat. As the worm bites into the meat, it is easily grabbed behind the head with fingers or pliers.

A little experience teaches the collector to pull out even large worms in one swift movement. Others hold the worm in one hand while they dig the bottom of it out of the sand with their other hand. If the worm resists, you simply wait a moment or two until it relaxes and then pull again. Otherwise you will only break off the head, which the worm will regenerate.

After capture beachworms can be kept alive for days. They should be washed carefully in sea water and dusted with fine sand so that each worm is completely coated and then put in a tin or wrapped in newspaper. Stored in a dry cool place, they will remain excellent bait for all fish of the surf zone. For small fish like whiting, the trick is to cover the bend and the shank of the hook but leave a small part of the hook point free. The worm will provide movement

Sea garfish,
Hemirhamphus
australis

Australian Bonito,
Sarda Chiliensis
australis

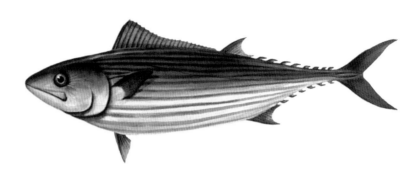

but for small fish the point of the hook needs to be clear. By using flattened hooks, you can thread the worm on to the line well above the hook. For bulky larger fish such as jewfish or mulloway, wrap the worm on the hook in a series of loops.

Pipis are avidly taken by fish of the surf and are outstanding bait because they will appeal to the quarry, but they quickly become soft and require skilful fishing. Batches of them are stranded on our beaches, immobilised and helpless, and easily gathered before the next wave sweeps in and gives them the chance to bury in the sand, moving down the beach to keep pace with the tide. Pipis are the main bait for many South Australians. Another shellfish that makes good bait is the black mussel, the organs of which have great appeal to many species. Open them up and you will find a large amount of flesh and slimy innards that are attractive to trevally, dart, parrot fish and red bream.

Greenweed is ideal for Luderick or blackfish and is available in bait and tackle shops but best gathered fresh from the rocks by the fishermen. Successful blackfish anglers learn to be very choosy about the weed they use and only collect it from sources known to be of a high standard. Some of the shops at the back of Botany Bay in Sydney specialise in supplying high class weed and have a ready market for it.

Greenweed or cabbage should not be stored in the sun or out in the wind and should never be cooked or soaked in freshwater. It can be dangled in saltwater or it can be spread on hessian bags soaked in

*The incomparable
yabbies, a superb
bait for most
popular species.*

saltwater. This will retain the milky smell and the minute marine creatures clinging to it.

Fishing inland, the angler will find that a good selection of baits is available. Nippers, the small green members of the prawn family found in freshwater streams, live in the mud under weeds on tidal flats and are collected by pudding around in the mud with your feet and raking them out alive. Like yabbies they have great appeal for saltwater species as well as inland varieties.

Yabbies are best collected by sucking them out of the sand with a yabby pump but old river men swear by their method of catching them dangling a piece of stale meat in the water on a piece of string. The yabbies attach themselves to the meat as they attack it and can easily be brought to the surface and collected in a scoop net Some anglers make themselves special yabby rakes, others prefer to drag prawn

nets across the bottom of known yabby waters. They are excellent bait and can be kept alive in a can of saltwater. The freshwater variety are really small crayfish that inhabit dams and bore drains. They form an appetising meal on their own but will cut up readily as bait for yellowbelly, redfin, trout and Murray cod.

For many anglers fishing with bait is a messy business which they prefer to discard in favour of lure fishing. A bewildering array of artificial lures are now on offer in tackle shops, many of them ingenious, some downright crazy, and fishermen have little trouble buying types that are effective and suit their budget. They fall into three basic categories, imitations, spinners and plugs. The imitations are copies, usually in plastic, of insects, squid, beetles and other creatures fish encounter, but this form lacks the popularity of plugs, spoons and spinners.

Spoons are mostly made of stainless

steel or copper and are intended to attract fish by creating an action in the water similar to another fish. They are available in singles, and doubles with treble hooks, dressed with furs and feathers or enamelled in bright colours. Give some thought to the retrieve you require before buying a spoon. They can cast, trolled or jigged at some depth, but their spinning action produces line twist if they are retrieved quickly. Hence they should be used with swivels and popular types like the Wonder Wobbler work best if they are slowly retrieved.

Spinners turn a full circle and mostly are blade-type lures painted in bright colours, with lots of holes and ridges. They are intended to attract fish where there is a moderate flow of water. For decades the aeroplane spinner was the universal favourite among Australian inland anglers, with blades mounted on a wire shaft

but separated by a bead or collar which whirred away with a sonic effect. Recently smaller, wobbler-lures like the Jensen Insects and the Celta have challenged the aeroplane spinner and built a good record against Macquarie perch, redfin and yellowbelly. They work better in rapids than in the still waters of lakes.

Skirted lures have proved extremely popular with game fishermen because they are easy to rig and come ina wide range of designs featuring feathers and plastic strips. They are the largest of all lures and aim to attract our biggest fish, with the skirt camouflaging large sharp hooks to deceive marlin and tuna. Make sure of the strength of the hook by lifting the skirt, as it is useless attracting billfish and other big fish if the hooks won't hold them. Knuckle-heads, Bulletheads, Bristle jig, Seven-seas Striker, Dickson Skirt, Konahead and Physchosquid can all be trolled well beyond the trail of the boat at fast speeds with telling effect.

Lures with bibs always attract attention in tackle shops, particularly those that can be adjusted according to the depth of water the angler plans to fish. The Rebel Fast Back, Bellbrook Midget, the Abu Killer, Shortland's Jointed Wobbler, Daiwa 453 and the Dickson range of flatfish and minnows are all proven lures, suitable for saltwater casting. Colour makes them look appealing in the shops but in the water size, shape and action is far more important.

Poppers with angles faced, cigar-shaped fizzers are ideal surface lures that can be trolled at high speeds. They can be retrieved quickly because of their slanted faces, but their success depends on the skill of the angler holding the rod. He has to make them pop, fizz or attract the attention of trevally, Spanish mackerel, albacore or bonito with rodwork that catches both water and air.

For all purpose inland fishing it is

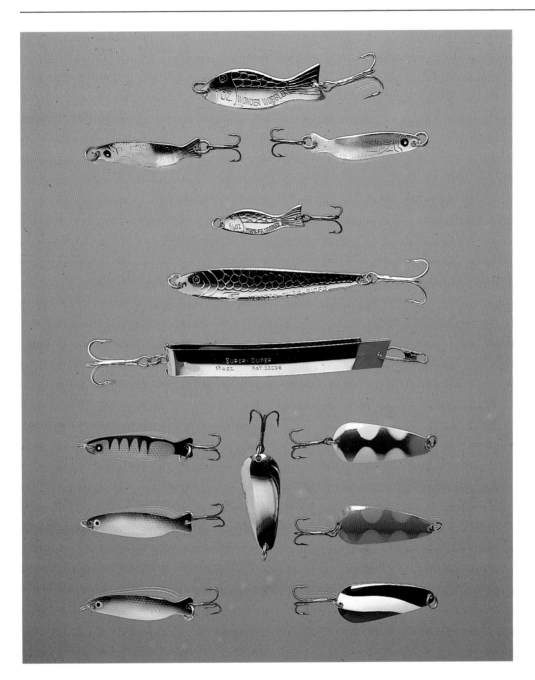

hard to go past the Flopy, the Arbogast Jitterbug or the Heddon Crazy Crawley. Some writers claim their success stems from the realistic manner in which they imitate stunned insects, others claim it is the action in the water that counts. Yet another group of commentators say they work because they simulate the movement of a crippled fish. The extraordinary thing is that they worked just as well as live baitfish, particularly in waters that have not seen such clever lures.

The Flopy often is referred to by the American term "plug," which is used to cover all lures that imitate insects, small fish and minnows. Plugs are designed to dive deep or skim along the surface. The Flopy can do both, depending on the presentation and the retrieve. Divers are the type with adjustable bibs, but Americans claim the most successful plugs are also fitted with internal rattles.

Regardless of whether your lures are fish-shaped, made of plastic, epoxy, metal, expensive wood or high-density Styrofoam they should suit the rod and lines to which they are fitted. They should be easily rigged or replaced and the rig has to be able to handle the fish the lure attracts. It is one of the great fascinations of sport fishing that the strangest lures often work as well as factory-crafted, artfully designed lures. Australian soldiers in New Guinea had great success luring fish with used cartridge cases. The best fish caught on Sydney Harbour during a contest for big prizemoney was taken by an angler who used a Mintie to lure a superb bream on to the hook.

CHAPTER THREE

Popular Species

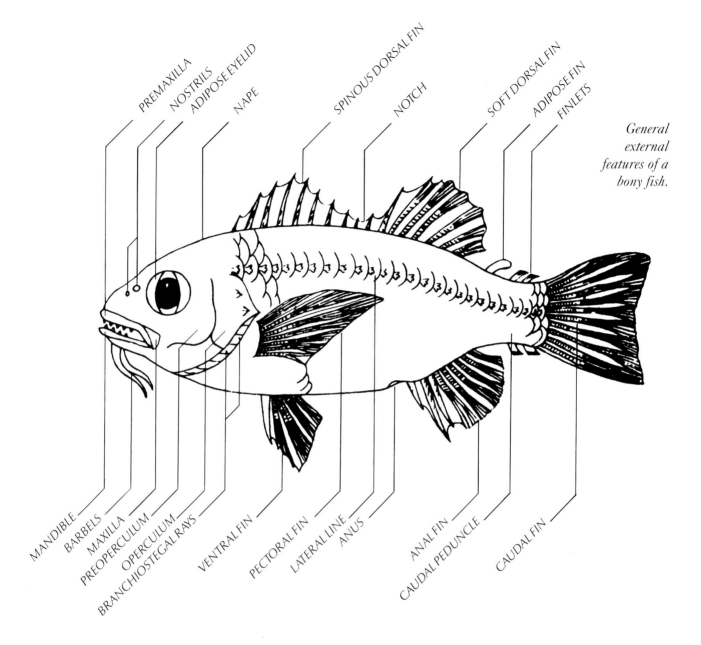

General external features of a bony fish.

Labels: PREMAXILLA, NOSTRILS, ADIPOSE EYELID, NAPE, SPINOUS DORSAL FIN, NOTCH, SOFT DORSAL FIN, ADIPOSE FIN, FINLETS, MANDIBLE, BARBELS, MAXILLA, PREOPERCULUM, OPERCULUM, BRANCHIOSTEGAL RAYS, VENTRAL FIN, PECTORAL FIN, LATERAL LINE, ANUS, ANAL FIN, CAUDAL PEDUNCLE, CAUDAL FIN

Scientists have so far identified more than 3,000 species of fish in Australian waters, 180 of them in freshwater, and more than 20 of them introduced from overseas. The fish heavily outnumber the experts studying their taxonomy and there is a great deal still to learn about a huge number of our species. This is understandable when the study of a single species can take years of work in the field, in laboratories, and in comparing sample specimens.

To cover Australia's entire fish population in a single volume would be impossible if all 3,000 fish had been thoroughly studied. Nor is it necessary in filling the needs of our sports fishermen as many of our fish are found in remote locations ar at depths amateur anglers never reach.

Far better to concentrate on the fish that are likely to turn up sometime in the average fishermen's lifetime, and ignore those that are too small or too big to ever be trapped on his lines. This narrows down the number of species, but it still leaves the difficulty of covering the chosen species distribution in some of the world's great oceans. For Australians fish in places washed by the Arafura Sea, the Coral Sea, the Tasman Sea, the Great Southern Ocean, the Indian Ocean, the Pacific Ocean and the Timor Sea. Their choice of locations ranges from the Great Barrier Reef, to Rottnest and the islands of Albrolhos, Exmouth Gulf, the Gulf of Carpentaria, from Bass Strait to Sydney Harbour, from Moreton Bay to Cairns, and hundreds more.

From the fish caught in all these saltwater locations, I have chosen those that most occupy amateur fishermen and have the greatest appeal to them as sport and on the table. The illustrations of these species are accompanied by summaries of their habits, recommended baits, tackle, the best methods of capture, and the lengths at which they may be legally taken.

In studying our favourite fish, it is intriguing to remember that many of them were named in the most haphazard manner. One was named after one of the crewmen in Governor Phillip's first fleet, others like the cods were named because they reminded settlers of fish back in Europe although they were not true members of the cod family. Australian salmon does not belong to the salmon family,

Australian bream have no relationship to European bream, which belong to the carp family Cyprinidae. The West Australian jewfish are not related to jewfish found in the eastern States, which go by the name of Mulloway. The Australian rock cod is not a cod but belongs to the world's 350 species of scorpionfish. The Queensland halibut is not a true halibut but belongs to the flatfish family that includes flounders and soles. A large number of fish we call perches are not perches at all.

From this short list of contradictions novices will wonder why Australia's fish names are so confusing. Part of the problem stems from the lack of a control authority before Federation, and part from the eagerness of State fisheries departments to go their own way. An attempt was made to introduce uniform fish names and after 16 years work a conference of experts from all States was held in 1963. The conference came up with some strange names. The fish known along the Australian east coast as the jewfish, dhufish in Western Australia, and elsewhere as butterfish was given the name mulloway. The fish known as queen snapper in some States and strongfish or red moki elsewhere was named morwong.

The experts knew they could not change the habits of a lifetime overnight and expected the list of uniform fish names to be adopted

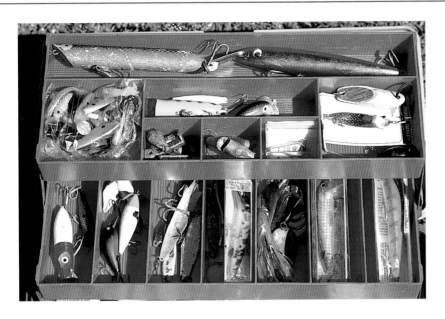

*A well equipped
tackle box.*

gradually. But 30 years later there is little sign of general acceptance of names like mulloway, which remains jewfish to the majority of anglers. Luderick are still niggers or blackfish to our rock fishermen. This is why the aliases of several of our best known species are provided.

HOW A FISH IS DESCRIBED

The bony fish is measured from the tip of the upper jaw to the typural point or the fold at the base of the tail when the fish is bent sideways. All bony fish have skeletons of pure bone whereas sharks, rays and sawfish have cartilaginous skeletons. The shape of a fish depends on the pressure of the water in which it lives and the action of the muscles that deposit calcium and influence bone formation. The scales are an important part of fish identification because they grow with the fish and form rings that indicate age. Scales may have their margins smooth (cycloid) or finely toothed (ctenoid).

Scales also assist in giving fish a silvery appearance by reflecting light, although the white or silver hue of the fish's belly is mainly due to the particles or a substance called guanin deposited in the skin. These particles are called iriodocytes because of their glitter. Experts describe fish by counting their scales along the lateral line and down the transverse line from the start of the dorsal fin to the centre of the belly. On fish like the herring which show no lateral line, the count is made between shoulder and tail where the line would otherwise occur.

Fins are swimming tools created from skin and muscle by the body of the young fish beating against the water. Distribution and positioning of the fins is also decided by muscular movement. Fish that wiggle or swim

Nannygai,
Centroberyx affinis

Red Gurnard,
Currupiscis kumu

with gentle wavy motions like flounder and sole have almost continuous fins around the body margin. In other fish these fins are restricted by areas of strong muscular action to the dorsal fin on the back of the fish and the anal fin of the underbelly. In some species a small adipose fin occurs behind the dorsal, which is itself often split in two. As well as these vertical fins, the majority of fish - but not all - grow two sets of paired fins, the pectorals and ventrals, set behind the gills one on either side of the body. The spines attached to fins are weapons, but the fins are mainly for propulsion. The colour of fish comes from nervous cells which spread pigment and allows fish to change colour if required, either for reasons of camouflage or merge into the background while they await prey.

NANNYGAI

are easily identified by their bright red colouring, red fins, large gold eyes, by the large gape of their mouths, and deeply forked tails. They have short deep bodies that average around 60cm in length and are conspicuous because of their red, violet and silvery reflections. They belong to the sawbelly or squirrel-fish family and are marketed as red snapper or redfish. They seldom exceed more than half a kilogram in weight. Few amateur anglers deliberately seek

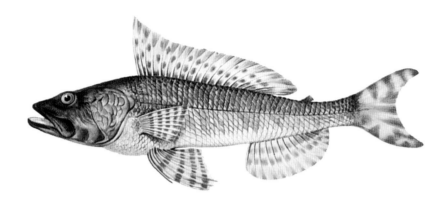

Sergeant Baker,
Latropiscis
purparissatus

them but they turn up regularly in the catches of offshore amateurs who bottom-fish reefs with pilchards, cut squid or prawn bait. They are fish of ancient lineage found in all Australian States but most plentiful in southern seas from Victoria, across the Great Australian Bight to Western Australia. The main varieties are the swallowtail nannygai, the Bight redfish and common nannygai.

RED GURNARDS

are fascinating fish who move along the ocean floor burrowing expertly for food, using their bony snouts to dig for sea worms and other scraps. They are often mistaken for flying fish because of their wing-shaped pectoral fins, but they use their wings to cling close to the bottom rather than for flying. They are found in all States, but are most abundant in Victoria, New South Wales, South Australia and Western Australia, where they are known as red rock cod. They are regularly caught by line fishermen in deep water, and are of good table quality after skinning. Some grunt or

groan as they are lifted from the water. Best known Australian species are the red gurnard, butterfly gurnard, flying gurnard, the spin gurnard and the sharp-beaked gurnard. In Western Australia, they are subject to a minimum legal length of 229mm, in South Australia 210mm. They reach 60cm, and 2kg, and require heavy sinkers to get baits down to where they live.

SERGEANT BAKER

are generally caught on snapper gear on lines of 9.07 breaking strain and 2/0 to 6/0 hooks. They bite on all cut fish, crustaceans and squid. They are attractively marked fish with bodies splashed in red, purple, crimson, yellow and orange. All their scales are edged in red and their tails are strongly forked and mottled in red and gold. They have heads like gurnards for whom they are often mistaken, and are the sole Australian representatives of a group of grinners and lizard fishes. They create high expectations when they are caught but once they are opened up emit a powerful odious smell. Their white

*Sailfish, Istiophorus
platypterus*

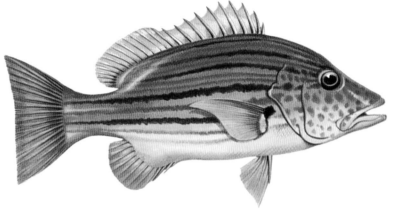

*Stripey, Lutjanus
carponotatus*

flesh is firm but few try their edible qualities because of the smell. They inhabit weeds and rocks in temperate seas in all States and in Western Australia can only be taken after they reach the 30cm legal length.

SAILFISH:

A member of Australia's billfish community, easily distinguished from marlin by their extraordinary sail-like dorsal fins. They are much smaller than marlin, lacking the depth of shoulder and body and unlike marlin remain in one area for extended periods. They are vividly blue from their sails down to their body lines, where they turn silver and white. Their large dorsal fins are freely sprinkled with black spots. Most of those taken in Australian seas average around 45 kg but they have been caught up to 79kg. Sailfish of world standard have been caught off Western Australia, New Guinea and Queensland, smaller specimens off New South Wales. They take the same fish baits and live fish as marlin and respond to feathered lures, but more are tagged and released on capture.

STRIPEY:

A confusing fish for anglers, as there are two fish in our seas that go under this name, one a member of the snapper family and the other a butterfly fish. The snapper-like stripey is the one with most appeal, roamers admired as panfish. they are plentiful along the Barrier Reef where they have a habit of darting in

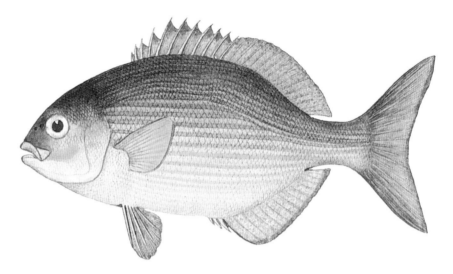

Low-finned Drummer

and out of coral, scattering the little fish on which they prey. They vary from red to reddish brown, with eight or more parallel bars running the length of their bodies. The fins are yellow. The stripe colour varies in the three States in which they are caught. They rise hungrily to trolled lures and most bottom baits.

LOW-FINNED DRUMMER:

One of a family of deep-bodied, fast-swimming fish highly esteemed for their fighting tenacity. The group includes the silver drummer, topsail drummer, southern drummer and the low-finned drummer, a Queensland variety that often falls to spearguns. They run fast and pugnaciously when hooked from their favoured habitat close to rocks, where they feed on algae, crabs and shellfish. Rock fish-ermen catch them on baits of cunjavoi, weed, prawns and shellfish, berleying them with breadcrumbs and bran. They need small but strong hooks, 4 to 1/0 and lines that can hold fish up to 12kg. Fishermen in boats

that can get in close to the rocks where the drummer lives do best with cabbage weed packed on their hooks.

NORTHERN BLUEFIN TUNA:

One of a group of fearless, stream-lined fish that can reach impressive speeds second only to marlin. Of the eleven tuna species in Australian waters, the northern bluefin favours the tropical and sub-tropical seas, but occasionally strays down as far as Eden on the New South Wales south coast. A number are taken in Western Australia as far south as Busselton. Like all Australian tunas, they wee originally known as tuny but the name was changed on discovery of a potentially lucrative United States market. The northern bluefin is similar in appearance to the southern bluefin but is more tapered in the body. They grow to 16kg and respond to pilchard, garfish, anchovy and cut fish baits and white or red feathered lures offered by trolling boats.

Spotted Whiting,
Sillaginodes punctatus

Trumpeter Whiting,
Sillago maculata

YELLOWFIN TUNA:

A superb fighting fish with a sickle-shaped pectoral fin that reaches back to the origin of the second dorsal fin. They attract a lot of game fishing boats along the Australian east coast, many of the boat centres on Port Stephens and Bermagui, and are taken frequently off Sydney. Most of those taken from boats weigh between 65kg and 90kg, but one taken off Bermagui by Harvey Howe in 1982 weighed 102kg. Their name is misleading because other tunas also have yellow fins and finlets. They are identified by the length of their pectoral fins, which extends well past the level of the second dorsal and back to the tail flukes in mature fish. They are caught at fast speed with whole live fish baits. Fine specimens have been caught at Lord Howe Island, in Queensland, Western Australia and Tasmania.

They are highly rated table fish, ideal for sashimi.

ALBACORE:

A beautifully streamlined fish which is one of the most prized of the tuna family because of its excellent table qualities. Most tuna fish is red but albacore meat is white. They are built for speed, from finlets to forked tails and have been timed at speeds up to 7km/h, and are an important part of the sport fishery from Port Stephens to Bermagui in New South Wales. An albacore weighing 21.60kg was taken off Narooma. They take all types of live fish and cut fish baits and usually are caught on light game tackle from trolling boats. A wire trace is obligatory.

Snapper, Pagrus auratus

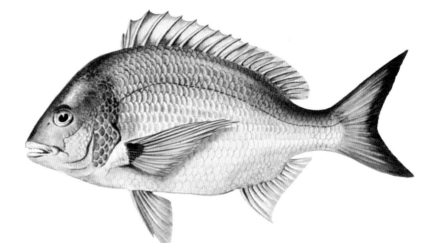

Yellow Fin Bream, Acanthropagrus australis

MULLOWAY:

One of the largest fish available to many anglers, growing to 60kg and 1.8 metres in length, but usually caught between 15 and 25kg. Universally known as jewfish, they turn up in harbours, estuaries, tidal rivers and surf. North of Rockhampton in the east and Carnarvon in the west they usually are replaced by their relatives, the spotted or blotched jewfish, and the silver jewfish, which is probably the best sport of the family. All mulloways can make a drumming, croaking noise by vibrating their air bladders. They go by a variety of names, including silver perch, grassy jew, banana jew and soapies, the name

for those with fur-like skins. They take baits and carry them for a while before swallowing so they need to be given free line at the strike. Baits of fresh whole fish, garfish, sea worms, pilchards and skinned octopus all work but they prefer live baits. Medium-sized fish are excellent eating.

KING GEORGE WHITING:

The largest of the eleven species whiting found in Australian waters, splendid table fare, found in waters from the south coast of New South Wales, around Victoria to South Australia and on to the southern coast of Western Australia. Also known as spotted whiting. The upper part of their light brown and golden bodies is liberally studded with small red or black spots. They usually require No. 1 to 4 hooks and bite best from November to February on baits of squid, pipi, cockles and small shell fish. They are very fast biters and one of the few fish in Australian waters that require alert response from anglers. Alot of whiting fishing is done on handlines with 1 to 3kg nylon lines. Threadline reels cope best with their quick strikes. Average size around 1kg.

TRUMPETER WHITING:

More discrimination in their choice of habitat than other whiting, but not as fussy in their taste in food. They are smaller and less striking in colour than King George whiting, with bodies varying from gold to light brown and a series of dark brown blotches on the back and sides. Most range from 150 to 350 grams and they school so densely catches between 80 and 100 are not unusual. Plentiful on offshore sand flats, they seldom penetrate large estuaries and tidal lakes. They are caught further from the shore than other whiting and commercial trawlers take big quantities of them.

SNAPPER:

Many boat fishermen concentrate solely on snapper because of their high quality as sporting fish of high table quality. They undergo several name changes as they mature from cockney bream, which spawn in sheltered waters in estuaries, bays and gulfs, to squire at the age of two, to school snapper in their third year, and finally when they go out to offshore reefs and develop crowns on their heads to old man snapper. They belong to a family with around 40 members, including tarwhine, pikey bream and sea bream and reach weights up to 20kg in their fully mature state. They are caught on king prawns, crabs, octopus, squid and cut fish. Wise anglers gut the first snapper caught and examine their stomach contents. Mature snapper have hard bony mouths that crush weak hooks, and need lines up to 9kg break strain. A rod and reel take more snapper than handlines. They are caught in southern Australia but prefer warmer water.

YELLOWFIN BREAM:

From a family known by a profusion of names, including emperor, pikey, red, butterfly, bluenose and government bream. The most common commercial and angling species are the yellowfin and black bream, which often produce hybrids in landlocked waters. They are one of our best table fish, very cunning, suspicious, and fitted with fine teeth that can rip and tear at food. They prefer the dark and seldom bite well in

Tarwhine,
Rhabdosargus sarba

moonlight. Noise easily scares them off. They mostly spawn in river mouths, maturing in their third year to 20cm and around 3kg. Yellowfin bream are caught on baits of shrimps, yabbies, sand worms, cut crabs and are most common from Gippsland Lakes to Townsville, with their populations overshadowing black bream.

TARWHINE:

A highly-rated member of the bream family, keenly sought as table fare, with a tell-tale silvery colour along the lower part of their bodies and longitudinal golden bands on the upper sides and back. The dorsal fin on their heads is golden brown. Along the Australian east coast tarwhine grow to 40cm and 2kg, but in South Australia tarwhine to 11kg have been recorded. Tarwhine fight doggedly for their size. In Victoria, small crabs appear the best bait, but in New South Wales small fish and marine worms usually succeed. In Queensland, they respond to fresh prawns and sea worms, in Western Australia to yabbies and worms, always fighting hard.

TERAGLIN:

Impressive relatives of the jewfish or mulloway family, with iridescent blue shoulders and silvery lower bodies and distinctive dark blotches behind the eyes and gill covers. They can be distinguished from jewfish by their tails, which always curve inwards. Mulloway tails curve outwards. The two species taken by anglers are the silver teraglin, also known s wire tooth or yankee whiting, and the common teraglin. They are restricted to the coastal waters of southern Queensland and the open coastal waters of New South Wales, whereas mulloway are found in all States. They do not enter harbours and remain offshore. Hungry "trags" hooked near the surface provide plenty of action. They can be berleyed to the surface from the reefs and gravel beds that they inhabit and take baits of squid, prawns, mullet, garfish and mackerel. At 80cm they are outstanding food fish.

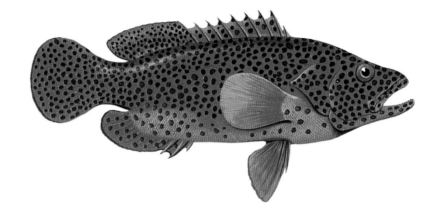

Coral Cod,
Cephalophilus
miniatus

Spotted Javelin,
Pomadasys hasta

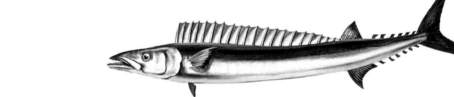

Barracouta,
Leionura atun

WESTERN JEWFISH:

The most prized fish in Western Australian waters which can be distinguished by their big heads, powerful mouths and the dark oblique bar that grows across the eyes to the interopercle. They have won the respect of anglers through a combination of outstanding fighting qualities and their table quality. they are caught up to 25kg in weight but the minimum legal length at which they can be caught is 50cm. A daily bag of ten Western Australian jewfish applies. They are taken with handlines or on rods and reels from rocks and boats with squid, prawns or small live fish baits. Off shore where the big ones live, they are unpredictable, but it is wise to give them plenty of line. Hooks attached to swivels are suggested. Distributed from Cape Naturalist to Shark Bay, but most abundant off Rottnest Island, the Albrolhos, Lucky Bay and Fremantle.

BROADBILL SWORDFISH:

A much prized billfish rarely caught by Australians, renowned for their wariness. Only small ones have so far been landed by our anglers and the much sought larger specimens continue to elude even the best-equipped game fishing boats. Swordfish catches are not uncommon in New Zealand, however, and they are regularly taken in Hawaii, California, Peru, Portugal and even inside the Mediterranean. The secret seems to be to adopt a completely different technique to that used on marlin, as they have very soft mouths. Baits need to be presented without any jerking. Swordfish bait is not trolled but kept until they are spotted.

CORAL COD:

A colourful fish, abundant right along the Great Barrier Reef, often caught by tourists from charter boats, the small fish on floating lines, larger ones on handlines. They are a strictly warm water fish that prefer the reef, the warm waters of Torres Strait, and northern Western Australia. They have striking red bodies covered in peacock-blue spots, with rounded tails that darken in maturity. They seldom grow beyond 450mm but are excellent table fish when skinned and filleted, with delicately flavoured firm white flesh. They bite on most baits, especially small fish and crustaceans and are often taken over snapper grounds.

SPOTTED JAVELIN:

The largest of Australia's javelin fish family, which inhabit semi-tropical waters and have a high rating among anglers because of their fighting abilities and excellent eating qualities. Spotted javelin fish grow to 5.5 kg and 65cm but are mostly caught around 3kg. The blotched javelin fish, a smaller and more abundant species, and the silver javelin, seen only in the far north, grow to 40cm. Spotted javelin are suckers for small spinners and plastic frogs and baits of live fish, prawns, small real frogs, pilchards and herring on 2/0 to 6/0 hooks. They are often confused with grunter because of their loud, croaking grunts on capture.

BARRACOUTA:

An outstanding sporting fish that has been known to leap into boats in pursuit of its prey. They inhabit the southern half of Australia and have been sighted in Bass Strait across to south-eastern South Australia, but no further north than Cape Moreton on the east coast. They provide plenty of excitement when trolled with light gear, though a growing number are caught from jetties and rocks with spinning gear. They are long and narrow in shape with large, flashing teeth, glittery steel blue above and silvery white below. The soft dorsal and the tail lobes are black edged. Unfortunately, they were misnamed by early settlers for they are not true

River Garfish,
Hamirhamphus
ardelio

barracuda, which are know in Australia as sea pike but belong to the same family as gemfish. Voracious feeders, they will pursue small live fish baits for hundreds of metres, and even in a boat fight so fiercely for their freedom it is customary to club them with a pick handle.

RIVER GARFISH:

One of the most plentiful Australian garfish known to biologists as "half-beaks." They feed among beds of sea grass in our rivers, estuaries and lakes and are also known as needle gars and splinter gars. River garfish are among 18 Australian varieties of garfish, most of them noted for their table quality and protruding beaks on the lower jaw. Anglers catch them as bait for larger fish or willingly cut through the large number of bones in their bodies to sample their flavoursome white flesh. They are calm weather sport, responsive to berley and take baits of chopped prawns, crabs or shellfish and stale bread.

RED ROCK COD:

One of the 80 species of the world's 350 varieties of scorpionfish, poorly rated as food fish because of the need

to get through their armour of sharp spines and fins. They have to be handled carefully as a sting from one can produce a burning sensation, slight paralysis, and swelling in the affected areas. Red rock cod have a bony strut or suborbital stay on their cheekbones, but are not strong swimmers. Nobody deliberately fishes for them but they are abundant off the Queensland, New South Wales and Tasmanian coasts. For those ready to take the trouble of boiling or barbecuing the meat after picking their way through all the bones and spines say these fish taste like good crab meat.

YELLOWBELLY FLOUNDER:

Fish of very high table quality, seldom taken by anglers unless they are equipped with flat-bottomed boats and spears. Some are caught by anglers who wade barefoot through the shallows with lights that tell them the flounders' whereabouts. They grow to 38cm, and cling close to the bottom, often almost disappearing in the sand, feeding on small sea worms, small shellfish and crustaceans. They are sometimes caught with light rods and small hooks baited with earth worms and fished on the bottom on rising

*Red Rock Cod or
Scorpion Cod,
Scorpaena cardinalis*

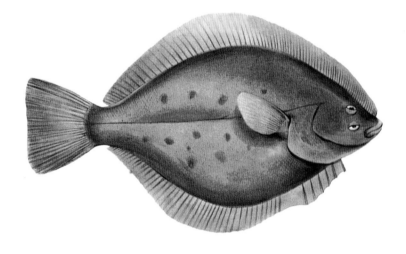

*Yellowbelly Flounder,
Rhombosolea tapirina*

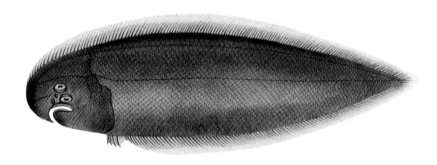

*Tongued Sole,
Cynoglossus bilineatus*

tides. Mostly, No. 1 hooks are enough.

TONGUED SOLE:

Often confused with their relatives, the flounders, sole have the same lifestyle and flattened bodies and the same eyes that move across to the right or left side of their bodies soon after birth. They are a gourmet's treat, but most of the varieties in Australian waters are not plentiful enough to market profitably. Tongued sole are easily distinguished from oval-shaped soles by their elongated bodies, which are similar in shape to an animal's tongue. best known of the tongued soles is the two-lined tongued sole,

Dolphin Fish,
Coryphaena hippurus

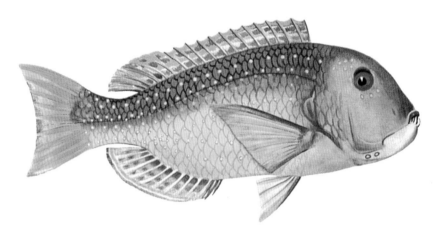

Venus Tuskfish,
Choerodon venustus

which grows to 40cm, and varies from sandy to brown in colour. They are all invariably white on the bottom side. All soles are carnivorous, existing on molluscs, crustaceans and sand worms. Born in rivers, they reach maturity in salt water.

DOLPHIN FISH:

An internationally admired blue-water speedster widely distributed throughout the world's oceans. Australia has two main species, both of which are described as dolphin fish to discriminate between them and the sea mammal of the same name. They are fish of exceptional speed which will dodge among the waves as they follow a trolled bait. They are

found only in warm water, maturing to around two metres in length and up to 35kg in weight. They have a characteristic long blue dorsal fin, bodies of blue, yellow and gold liberally sprinkled with green and blue spots, with wide, forked tails. Dolphin fish attacking a lure light up in a glowing show of colour. Wire traces are recommended because of their powerful mouths with a swivel to curb tangled lines in the fight. The older dolphin fish get, the blunter their heads become.

VENUS TUSK FISH:

A colourful member of the wrasse family which inhabit coral reefs, big , pugnacious fish that have to be

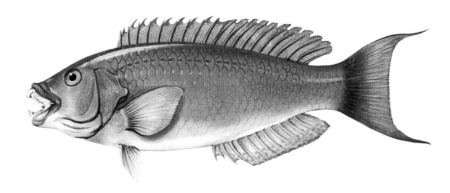

*Scarlet Parrotfish,
Pseudolabrus
coccineus*

*Bonefish,
Albula vulpes*

turned quickly before they reach the safety of crevices or underwater caves where they can break the line. They are greenish-grey above the head, purple along the top of their bodies but become bright pink on the sides. The young have slightly curved tails which become square-cut in adults. All the fins are edged in light blue, with a touch of gold. They average 900 grams in weight but venus tusk fish to 4.5 kg have been rod-fished on Cape Moreton reefs in southern Queensland. They like cut fish baits.

They have small mouths and rarely change their coral diet and because of this are seldom taken by anglers. The scarlet parrotfish is one of the most plentiful of the group which includes six-banded parrotfish, surf parrotfish, blue-barred parrotfish and rosy parrotfish. They have a marked preference for shallow water. Some anglers believe they are partial to baits of ghost crabs and consider them good table fare, provided they are cleaned and iced or cooked soon after capture to avoid them becoming mushy.

SCARLET PARROTFISH:

An appealing, vividly coloured family of coral chewing reef fish often mistakenly grouped with wrasses.

DUSKY FLATHEAD:

One of the largest of Australia's 40-odd species of flathead, with small, needle-sharp teeth, and nasty spines.

Experienced anglers stab duskies through the head with a knife or stamp their boots on the duskies head to dodge a painful sting from the spines as they remove the hook. Duskies reach 1.2kg in length, and fall to chain hooked rigs that hold the bait clear of the bottom, or anglers with two-metre spinning rods using lures like the ABU shiner, killer or swaybacks. Live bait should be firmly attached to hooks.

BONEFISH:

A badly neglected fish among Australian anglers, but highly prized overseas. Part of the cause of its lack of recognition here is that it is very difficult to catch, usually because anglers are unaware of it habits. Bonefish are very fast, suspicious fish of tropical shallows ranked by experts like Zane Grey and Ernest Hemingway as the greatest speedster in the sea. There are authentic accounts of bonefish taking out 350 metres of line on their first run. Yet they grow to only 7.5 kg and the world record stands at 8.6kg. Frequently confused with sand whiting, bonefish have only one dorsal fin, whiting two. Mouths of bonefish are underslung, located near the snout tip. They are bright green to blue above with silvery sides. They demand sharp hooks and should be quietly stalked on squid, worms, ghost crabs and pilchard baits.

TAILOR:

A popular light-game fish on all the Australian coasts south of the Tropic of Capricorn. They school in large numbers and provide sport for a large number of admirers. When the tailor are running they gorge themselves in their feeding frenzies, moving in to chop through schools of mullet and pilchard with their sharp teeth, biting powerfully and vigorously. They show the same tenacity when hooked and usually continue to fight after they have been lifted from the water. They are pale green to bluish on top, silvery below with olive-green to white fins that propel them through the water at speeds rare in fish or around 10kg when mature. Despite their bite, they have soft mouths and need to be brought on board before they have a chance to chop at the line. Wire traces and ganged hooks work best with baits of garfish, yellowtail and bonito.

LUDERICK:

Vegetarians of many aliases, always found close to rocks, reefs, piers and other places where weed grows. They have a great taste for the stuff and can often strip a hook of weed that has been clumsily attached. They are known in New Zealand as parore and in Australia as niggers, darkies, blackfish, black bream, rock perch and many other names. Hardly anybody but scientists calls them luderick. Whatever their names, they have a vast following among sports

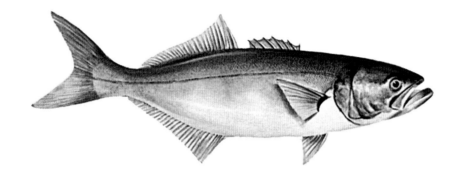

Tailor, Pomatomus saltator

Dusky Flathead, Planiplora fusca

fishermen who rate them among the gamest fish in our seas. Weed is the sole effective bait, according to life-time nigger fishermen, but they will take squirt worms, pipis, cunje and peeled prawns. They fall to a variety of hook patterns, but hooks should be small, with flattened snecks because of their small mouths.

ROCK BLACKFISH:

A popular sporting fish in New South Wales, the only State in which they are found, also known as pigfish and black drummer. They are often taken by anglers fishing for silver drummer. Their flesh is firm and white and tender if eaten soon after capture. Their maximum weight and length is unknown because they are so often confused with drummer, but long-time anglers are inclined to set their biggest weight at 6kg. They are very

dark, bluish-black fish with longitudinal stripes along their backs. They take baits of crab meat, fish flesh, prawns and cunje but feed mainly on weed. They are very powerful swimmers that need to be turned quickly before they reach hideouts in rocky crevices.

SILVER DRUMMER:

Another weed-eater that can some-times be tempted by fish, squid, prawn and crab meat baits offered on handlines. They inhabit rocky spots where there is plenty of movement in the water, with specimens between 3.5 and 4.5 kg offering good sport. Silver drummer are thought to be a mainly New South Wales fish, but they are common in South Australia and Western Australia, where they are known as buffalo bream. They are renowned tackle-

John Dory,
Zeus faber

busters and appear to reach larger sizes in the west. In the eat silver drummer lose their edible quality in larger sizes. A related species caught in Norfolk Island and Lord Howe Island is said to cause nightmares. It is known as the dream fish.

AUSTRALIAN SALMON:

A wonderful sporting fish but not a true salmon. They belong to a perch family which has only two members in Australian waters, the western salmon and the eastern salmon. They are abundant fish which fight with great dash and stamina and grow to a weight of around 9kg, but are poor pan fish. Commercial fishermen reserve them for canning. Few fish match their tenacity or their exciting acrobatics when hooked, either by spinning in the surf or trolling from boats. In the east they bite best on beach worms and pipis, in the west on pilchards. Both Australian species

undertake long migratory journeys and amateur fishermen eagerly seek news of them when the big schools are due. In Western Australia juvenile salmon schools assemble on the south coast before migrating right across the bottom of Australia. They cut through nylon lines so often it is necessary to use linked carlisle hooks with the point exposed so that the salmon cannot remove the bait without being hooked.

JOHN DORY:

The best known of the nine dory families found in Australian waters, all of them ugly-looking fish with capacious mouths which they can extend with remarkable speed when they sight food. They are surface or bottom fish of offshore reefs, caught in large numbers by spearmen and on handlines. King dories are the largest member of the family but John dory are the most celebrated because of

Red Emperor,
Lutjanus sebae

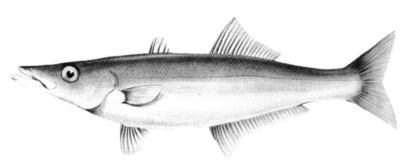

Long-finned Seapike,
Dinolestes lewini

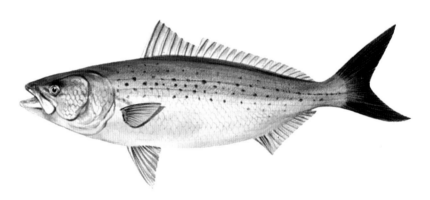

Australian Salmon,
Arripis trutta

the black spot on their golden yellow bodies and their great reputation as food fish. Their flesh is firm and white and fillets easily. John dory have soft mouths best presented with single hooks no bigger than 2/0 to 4/0. Silver dory and mirror dory have similar fingermarks on their torsos, but these are very faint compared with the large dark spot on John dory.

YELLOW LEATHER JACKET:

The largest of the 50 species of leatherjacket, also known as Chinamen leatherjacket spread around Australia. They grow to 70cm but are mostly caught around 45cm. Their skin is very rough and it is wise to wear gloves when handling them. They are easily identified through their completely yellow sides and slightly brown backs. They are such voracious feeders, traps containing baits only have to be lowered a metre or two over the side before they are returned to the boat with several yellow jackets kicking about in them. Australia is among the few countries in the world where leatherjackets are eaten because some of the overseas varieties are poisonous.

MUDSKIPPER:

Intriguing little gobies that grow to 100mm which skip about mudflats at surprising speed at low tide, searching for small crustaceans and insects. There are eleven species in Australian waters, where they are also known by a variety of local names such as johnny jumpers, climbing fish, and goggle-eyed mangrove fish. They have been described by scientists as piscatorial paradoxes, fish that drown if they spend too much time under water. Mud skippers often will lie motionless in the mud for several minutes before taking off in dramatic skittering runs. They are both carnivorous and quarrelsome, and there is no point in trying to catch them. It's more fun just to watch them climb over rocks and roots and trunks of mangroves, showing eyes like periscopes.

RED EMPEROR:

This fish, known throughout the Barrier Reef as the red emperor, is not an emperor at all but a sea perch. They are one of the most prized fish in Queensland waters, growing to 22kg, fighting pugnaciously when hooked, and providing an outstanding meal even in the larger sizes. They are caught on everything from octopus to cut fish. They are fish of warm tropical waters found right across the north of Australia into the Indian Ocean. The best catches are made by berleying them up from the bottom of coral reefs, where they can be taken on handlines. They have to be brought in promptly or they will dart back into coral hideouts. Best rigs are those that take sinkers down, with swivels to restrict twist in the line.

LONG-FINNED SEA PIKE:

Robust fish with elongate profiles, cylindrical torsos, and large mouths full of canine teeth. They are golden brown on top, silvery below, and reach a length of 50cm. The large gape in their mouths extends almost to their eyes and the lower jaw is longer than the upper jaw. Both the head and body are covered by cyclid scales. Long-finned pike are not related to European pike, which are freshwater fish, and should not be confused with the yellow-finned sea pike or snook, which have similar heads. They are splendid sporting both renowned speedsters, and their long tapered bodies give them the edge over queenfish and dolphin fish. They strike lures at breathtaking speed and their first run strips a lot of lines, but they are loners who intercept baits and lures intended for marlin. Highly rated as table fish, they can bite bait fish in half with a barely perceptible slash of their needle-sharp teeth. Navy blue above, fading to a silvery platinum colour below, with 20 odd olive or blue cross bars right along the body. The snout is extended. they often cripple their food by cutting off the tail and then eating the remainder. Wahoo grow to 1.8 metres but are mostly caught around 14 and 18kg. They will take high speed drones and similar lures and baits of pilchard, bonito, whole mullet and garfish, but the hooks need to be set well back in the bait.

GOLDEN TREVALLY:

One of the most attractive of Australia's 60 species of trevally, and the best eating of all the trevallies. They are found in tropical and temperate waters, but sometimes venture south to Tasmania and across the South Australian coast to Western Australia. Juvenile golden trevally are a brilliant gold colour with ten or more well defined vertical stripes across the shoulders and back. As they mature the glow in their colour fades and the dark bars fade, although the fins retain their golden hue. They reach 1.2 metres in length

and up to 35kg in weight and specimens in the higher weights lack the stripes. They are taken with strip baits, crustaceans and plugs. They fight pugnaciously when hooked, and on death the golden colours of their youth and the dark bands vividly reappear for a few minutes.

PAINTED SWEETLIPS:

One of a colourful group of sea perches found mainly in the tropical waters of Queensland and the Northern Territory, which occasionally stray as far south as Cape Moreton. they belong to the same family as the emperors. They are usually taken in numbers at night by berleying them up from the bottom of coral reefs and are easily caught on handlines, though they fight strongly when hooked. Best rigs are those that allow baits to swing free as sinkers take the bait down. Sweetlips grow to 18kg but are usually caught at around 2.5 to 5kg. Both juveniles and mature fish retain the same splendid flavour. They are brown on top with a dark longitudinal line right down the body, lighter below, but with dozens of gold, orange and black spots sprinkled over their entire torso.

ROCK WHITING:

A member of the wrasse family also known as grass whiting and stranger, which prefers temperate waters in Australia. They have a lengthy dorsal fin, characteristic of the wrasse

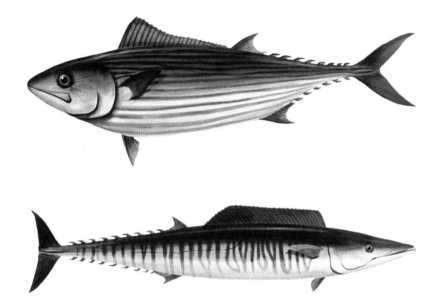

Australian Bonito,
Sarda chiliensis
australis

Wahoo,
Acanthocybium
solandri

fish which will leap clear of the water when hooked on light tackle. Small sea pike are outstanding bait for Spanish mackerel. They make strong runs with the bait and need to be brought in before they have a chance to slash through the line with those sharp teeth. They are mostly caught by trolling, some on jiggled strip bait by anglers using ganed hooks.

AUSTRALIAN BONITO:

Fast, pugnacious small tuna that habitually broach the ocean surface to feed on shoals of anchovies, pilchards and hardy-heads. They are also known as skipjacks, horse mackerel and skippers. They offer anglers splendid sport on light tackle and make ideal bait for sharks, marlin, sailfish and big tuna. They average around 5kg but have been taken up to 7.5kg off Bermagui. They are readily identified by their bluish bodies and the ten or more stripes that run right along the sides, with those near the belly tending to break into wider bars.Leaping bonito have a combination of spots and broken bars on top and continuous stripes along the bottom. Striped bonito have only five stripes below the lateral line. They take most baits offered by trolling boats but are particularly partial to small live fish. They are abundant on the east coast and are occasionally taken in Victoria waters but have not been recorded elsewhere.

WAHOO:

An outstanding game fish that has thrilled many fishermen with its speed and stubborn fighting qualities, often jumping clear of the sea in their efforts to get free. They are faster than Spanish mackerel or barracuda,

Golden Travally,
Gnathanondon
speciosus

Painted Sweetlips,
Plectorhinchus pictus

Rock Whiting,
Haletta semifasciata

family, and an elastic mouth in which the teeth are fused to form a parrot-like beak. They are bright greenish blue on the back, shading to a light silvery colour below, and their bodies are covered in a network of golden lines. There are ten indefinite black bars on the sides, and a large dark spot behind the mid-point of the dorsal fin. Rock whiting are found from New South Wales around to Western Australia, with the biggest quantities taken in Tasmania and South Australia. They are present at the lower end of the Barrier Reef but are overshadowed there by more challenging sportfish. Amateurs take them from inshore rocks, over coastal

Red Morwong,
Morwong fuscus

Tasmanian
Trumpeter,
Latris lineata

reefs on fresh weed.

RED MORWONG:

A fascinating member of the deep-bodied morwong group which dwell in Australia's temperate and cold waters. Red Morwong are often captured by spear or line along the New South Wales coast and to a lesser extent in Queensland. Like the rest of their family they have blubberlips, and are bright reddish-brown across their backs and upper bodies, turning to salmon pink or silver along the belly. A bright red network like mesh wire overlies their bodies, an effect created by the edging to the body scales. The eyes

are set in an irregular orange patch. They grow to a weight of 3kg and are fishing in fairly shallow inshore coastal reefs on baits of crabs and prawns. They often form into schools that attract spear fishermen and underwater photographers. They are first-rate table fare.

TASMANIAN STRIPED TRUMPETER:

One of the best known Australian members of the trumpeter group which have been reported at weight up to 26kg, and lengths of 1.3 metres. They are deeply-bronzed fish eagerly sought by gourmets because of their superb flavour. They are closely related to our two species of bastard trumpeter and have very similar eating habits and distribution. But bastard trumpeter lack the stripes that carry right along the body of Tasmanian trumpeter. They are predominantly brown in colour and pink below with deeply forked tails, whereas bastard trumpeter are dark olive-green in colour. They feed at night and avoid handlines, and are mostly taken by spearmen. A few succumb to anglers using long shanked hooks, and baits of squid, octopus and molluscs. The best catches are taken offshore on snapper rigs.

RAINBOW RUNNER:

Powerful streamlined fish of the open seas distributed throughout the world's tropical waters. They grow to 1.3 metres in length and are highly rated as sport fish and provide delectable meals. Japanese gourmets prepare special sauces when they eat rainbow runner. They are built for speed with slim, elongated bodies and magnificent crescent-shaped tails. They are mainly fished on the fringes of the Barrier Reef where they are a favoured trolled bait for giant marlin. They are deep green to pearly blue on top, silvery along the belly, with bright blue narrow stripes edged in yellow between. They reach 4.7kg

in Australian waters but have been taken at double that weight overseas. They are mostly trolled on feathered jigs which stay near the surface.

TURRUM:

Important game fish of incredible stamina which have contributed a lot to the reputation of Cairns as a game fishing centre. They belong to the great trevally family and have earned the respect of anglers for their tenacious fighting qualities. Built for a scrap, they have very powerful, compressed bodies and deeply forked tails, milky blue on top, silvery around the belly, with up to six vertical bands across their bodies in the form of brown or black dots. They are also known as golden trevally and are confused with their relatives the giant trevally. Turrum are mostly taken trolling from game boats, with baits of cut fish, live garfish, squid and prawns and also bite on spoons and drones. They usually strike without being seen in a series of deep lunges and tire slowly, testing the patience of anglers unfamiliar with their guile. They need lines of at least 27.21kg breaking strain and 6/0 to 8/0 hooks, and even with linked hooks and wire traces it often takes half an hour to land them.

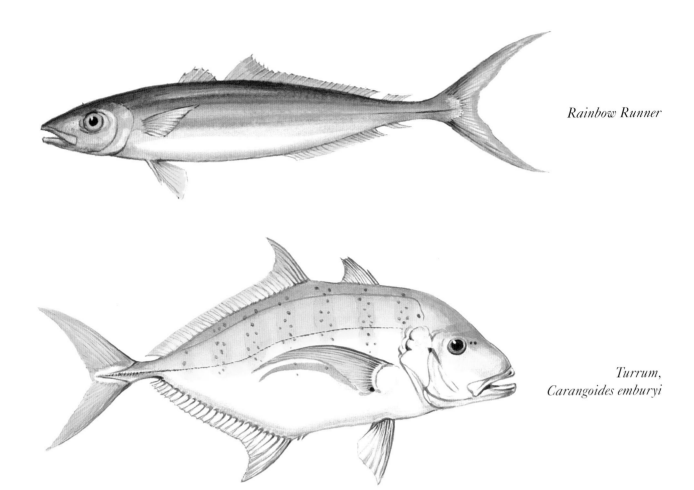

Rainbow Runner

Turrum,
Carangoides emburyi

CHAPTER FOUR

Freshwater Fishing

Australia's freshwater rivers, dams and lakes offer rewarding fishing, but it often takes a little trouble to find it. Unlike the oceans, estuaries and bays enjoyed by most of the population, our rivers are often disappointing venues for fishing excursions. The range of fish species is restricted, the flow of water which brings great fishing riches overseas is missing, and our river systems are often excessively hot, and badly affected by drought.

The days of great hauls of Murray cod have gone, but in the far north where the barramundi reigns supreme and in the colder regions of the Snowy Mountains system and in most of Tasmania there is still good prospects for an outstanding fishing outing. Government hatcheries and acclimatisation societies are doing a fine job with re-stocking programmes.

Lake Eucumbene, which holds nine times as much water as Sydney Harbour remains our most popular trout fishing spot, and the filling and breeding of fish for other dams in the system, Jindabyne, Jounama, Blowering and Talbingo has prospered. Down stream reaches often produce splendid trout because the cold water released from these dams provide ideal trout water.

Trout remain the big success of the 20 odd species of fish introduced into Australia. They provide excellent sport on unweighted baits and artificial spoons and lures, but the genuine trout angler sticks to wet or dry flies and usually ties them himself. These are the sportsmen who release many of the trout they catch, preferring to take only what they need for the table and refusing to come away heavily laden with fish.

Presentation is the key to trout fishing and to master it requires regular practice. Most alpine regions offer accommodation these days with a guide or tutor on hand to assist beginners. It is a sound investment for trout fishing can be a consuming passion and it it infuriating to be in the right place to catch trout only to be let down by your inability to cast and retrieve.

Fishing from a bank is probably the best way to start but a little practice in your backyard swimming pool before you leave home will not go astray. Start by trying to master casting over short distances and gradually extend your casts as your confidence grows. Good trout water usually runs through somebody's property and from the start it pays to get into the habit of politely seeking permission to go through, leaving gates and fences as you find them.

The time of year and time of day in which you go trout fishing dictates your tactics as you need to get your lures further out and deeper when trout are not feeding. When they begin to feed they are near the surface and you must vary your cast

Recommended Australian Trout Flies (L to R):

Top, *Glenn Innes Grasshopper, Mrs Simpson, Hamil's Killer, Black Phantom;*

Centre, *Parson's Glory, Lord's Killer, Fuzzy Wuzzy, Fuzzy Wuzzy;*

Below, *Dorothy, Dingo, Craig Nighttime, Tailape Tickler.*

accordingly. Take care that the trout do not see you and watch the way veteran tour anglers mask their presence by stooping or ducking away from river banks. Avoid stamping your feet or being silhouetted against the sky.

Trolling is one of the best methods of catching trout and most of our inland species. Don't pay out too much line for successful trolling as your lures do not need to go down very deep and are more likely to attract fish if you can dance the lure over the surface. Keep your boat speed down. Spoons and swimming plugs only need to dip a metre down and even the deep-diving trout plugs never run down more than three metres. The colder months between May and October are best for trolling

as the fish are more likely to swim near the surface. Once the weather hots up from November to February the water will not be as clear and it is then that the big, coloured blades that make plenty of underwater noise are successful.

It is important to study the area where you are fishing and try to work out where the fish will be concealed. They like to be out of the sun in the shade so look for fallen trees or overhanging foliage or sunken logs. These are the places where trout are likely to be, particularly if there is a current running nearby which will bring them scraps of food. Cast up past the reeds or boulders where you think they may be hiding.

Apart from trout Australian inland waters offer splendid fishing for

Atlantic salmon, Murray cod, silver and golden perch and redfin in southern States. Up north, as well as barramundi, mangrove jack, saratoga, spangled grunter, Barcoo grunter, the English wyandotts or yellowtail grunter, sooty grunter, red bass, catfish, freshwater mullet and several lesser known gudgeons dominate freshwater anglers' attention. But several other species bob up occasionally, such as the sleepy cod, the hair-back herring, the primitive archer fish, and the freshwater long tom. One long tom was caught 200 kilometres from the nearest tidal water. Like the hair-back herring, freshwater long toms will take lures and wet flies.

Perhaps the most exciting of the northern species is the tarpon. Anglers expect a tough fight when they hook a barramundi but few of them are prepared for the tenacious battle tarpon put up to throw the hook. They are often airborne in the fight for freedom and pound for pound offer better sport than any other species.

Grunters in the north are seldom timid despite their generally small size and will take either flies or spinners. Striped grunters have been taken in most tropical streams and in clear water often swim close to the angler. Black and sooty grunters will take a bait, spinner, spoon, fly or wobbler and they usually fully test the fisherman's gear.

Baiting A Hook

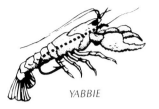

YABBIE

GRASSHOPPER

MUDEYE

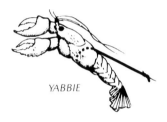

YABBIE

BLACK CRICKET

MINNOW

WORM

A very happy angler with his Salmon.

Although the clear water they favour often disappears the "silver bream" of the Murray-Darling system, more correctly known as the silver perch, rewarded anglers for years as a fighting fish and splendid table fare. They make the typical grunter noise when distressed and will take lures. Another grunter that fights impressively is the Ord River grunter, often wrongly identified as a mangrove jack.

The most famous fish of the north, however, is unquestionably the barramundi, a giant perch that can destroy expensive tackle and has an unrivalled reputation as a table fish. Government experts tried to have the name "Giant Palmer Perch" accepted when the uniform names conferences were held in the 1960s, but there was such an outcry from professionals who market this delectable fish the government conceded defeat and reverted to barramundi, an old aboriginal name. Official attempts to have only the Dawson River saratoga known as barramundi failed and ended up with two fish being referred to as barramundi.

The barramundi is so important to Queensland's economy that a closed

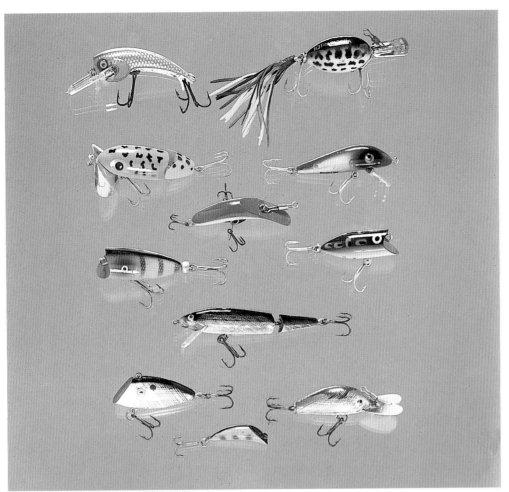

Ideal Freshwater Lures (L to R):

Top, an Arbo-gaster, Flopy, Tiger and a Jitterbug, Daiwa Diver, Jitterbug and a Tiny Lucky, a Jointed-Minnow, Red Flasher and a Canadian Wriggler, and a Red 250.

season was introduced during their late summer breeding season. This has had the effect of protecting the barramundi when it moves down to spawn in river mouths and estuaries in saltwater. The fertilised eggs are then carried away into freshwater. Theo Roughley fixed the maximum size of barramundi in Australia at 52.17kg or 120lb, but emphasised that one had been caught in the Bay of Bengal that weighed 252.12kg or 580lb. This is very misleading for amateur fishermen who are unlikely to encounter barramundi beyond 10kg as they often use tackle that is far too heavy for the average catches. Barramundi strike with explosive force on a wide range of lures,

spinners and are particularly partial to bellbrooks. They demand plenty of line but 9.07 breaking strain is enough.

Another prized freshwater fish Australians welcome on the table is the Atlantic salmon, a much-prized sporting fish introduced to this country in 1963 and now bred in cages off Tasmania. The Atlantic salmon in Burrignjuck Dam and Lake Jindabyne depend on regular restocking from government hatcheries for their survival, but in the sea they reach very large sizes. Atlantic salmon strike trout flies after mouthing it. Unlike trout they become more interested each time the cast falls near them, but the inland variety in Australia, locked in and unable to get to the sea, are sullen fish that do not leap high out of the water like their American counterparts and seldom weigh more than 3kg.

A far larger inland species is the legendary Murray cod, which have been recorded in weights approaching 80kg and 1.8 metres in length. Despite their great bulk, they are fish of delicious flavour, but sadly depleted by over-fishing. They are still taken commercially in some States although they do not provide the abundant cash returns they once did. They require heavy tackle. Efforts to introduce Murray cod in Western Australia failed, but they appear to survive extreme heat and drought in Victoria, South Australia, New South Wales and even into Queensland.

Some fascinating research has recently established that Trout cod, Clarence River cod and Mary River cod, are all separate species. Previously it was thought these were colder weather versions or the undeveloped Murray cod. They may all have belonged to the same family centuries ago, but long isolation in their own habitat has produced characteristics in the three other cods which justifies biologists classifying them separately.

CHAPTER FIVE

Rigs That Work

When the fish are feeding, anglers on crowded beaches catch most fish if they can cast accurately out beyond the first line of breakers.

Sports fishermen have devised a vast selection of rigs in which they arrange hooks, sinkers, rigs, swivels, floats and anti-twist devices at the end of their lines to tempt the fish and overcome testing conditions. Rigs have always formed an integral part of fishing with families handing down combinations that work from one generation to another. Well chosen rigs can often take the bait or lures to the fish despite heavy swells, nasty winds or unco-operative tides.

The experts who have made a lifetime study of this intriguing part of the fisherman's repertoire believe there are only a few basic methods, however, and that all the hundreds of others are only variations of these old forms. The only likely change in effective rigs comes with the arrival of improved equipment. The change from cord to nylon lines, for example, had a marked effect on rigs and the improvement in the engineering of small but vital things like swivels and rings has also brought advances.

In choosing a rig, consider the type of fishing in which they will be used. Rigs for the beach, for the rocks, for bays and estuaries, saltwater lakes, deep sea and freshwater dams all vary, just as they do for trolling and spinning. Successful barleying to attract and hold fish in an area should also be supported by rigs that take the bait to them. Leatherjackets that bite through 14kg nylon with great ease, sand crabs that attack baits, and other predators can all be thwarted by certain rigs.

A few basic rules apply whatever the rig: nylon traces or leaders should be of a lighter breaking strain than the main line, swivel sizes should be kept as small as possible, discard any rig in which the hooks are likely to catch in the brass rings, and always remember that sinkers are fundamentally of two kinds, fixed or running. The best running sinkers are those that are free to travel along the line and permit the fish to mouth, swallow and swim off with the bait without arousing its natural caution. But running sinkers are seldom practical when beach fishing. major advances in rod-making has virtually ended the need for very heavy lines when rock fishing. Few fish caught from the rocks can break today's rod and reel fitted with matching line of 7kg breaking strain.

thick with barnacles or other obstruction, a wire trace is recommended.

BEACH FISHING RIGS:

Sinker weights play a vital role in this form of fishing. The weight varies according to the conditions and the breaking strain of the line being used. Distance will be shortened if the line is too heavy for the sinker, and the line may be lost through breakage if the sinker is too heavy for it. Styles of sinkers vary considerably

ROCK FISHING RIGS:

"Bobby corking" remains one of the most practical forms of rock fishing, with running floats facilitating distance casting and adding accuracy, an essential factor in fishing confined areas. The cork is slit vertically in the centre with a sharp knife and the line forced into the slit. In shallow water additional lead probably will not be needed but when casting weight is required a lead tube can be fitted into the cork.

Expert Dick Lewers advocated the use of a tennis ball float as this will contract the line and eliminate the need for a stopper. For locations

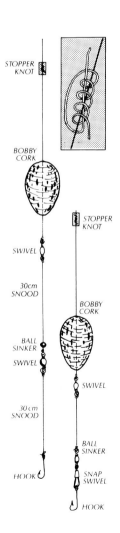

Running bobby cork rigs for sidecast reels.

but the running helmet and the running ball sinkers are popular in all States. The ball sinker does not roll across the sand as many anglers believe, but tends to bury in the sand; the current is the main factor in moving a rig along a beach. Beach rods should be inspected regularly for wear against the tip guide in the initial stages of the cast.

RIGS FOR BAY AND ESTUARY:

Anglers generally use far lighter tackle in the calmer waters of bays and estuaries than in places pounded by the waves. Perched on jetties, bridges and wharves, their main considerations are the estuarine tides and currents. Smaller fish are the target, some of them like bream of timid disposition compared to their relatives in the surf who do not hesitate in attacking baits.

Bream, garfish, mullet, ruff, flounder, bass, whiting, sole and tarwhine respond to float fishing and lately have been shown to take flies. Whatever rig you choose, barley will increase your prospects of good catches, with the methods of releasing scraps of food open to wide choice.

RIGS FOR SALTWATER LAKES:

Australia is liberally studded with vast areas of saltwater which are cut off from the ocean for a large part of the year, and in some places dynamiting has to be used to free water locked in by sand bars. Fly fishing in these areas unaffected by tides or currents has become increasingly popular. Barleying always helps.

RIGS FOR FRESHWATER LAKES AND DAMS:

Light tackle suits the normally calm waters of our inland lakes and dams, and today's threadline reels achieve the casting distance normally required, regardless of whether the angler operates from a boat or the shore. The main problems are the winds that blow in towards the water's edge. The rig shown provides a simple way of overcoming the problem with bubble or float.

RIGS FOR DEEP SEAS FISHING:

In rigging for fishing at sea, the anglers problems are depth and current or a combination of these. Heavy sinkers are the only answer and sinkers between 224 grams and 453 grams are often used. Traces should be lighter for both the hook and sinker than the main line, particularly over reefs. This way if either becomes fouled and a break-off is necessary, the main line remains intact. It is important in fishing from the same boat as several other anglers if you all use the same line size. It will prevent arguments if the lines are swept into each other and a tangle results.

CHAPTER SIX

Preparing Fish for the Pan

SKINNING A FISH

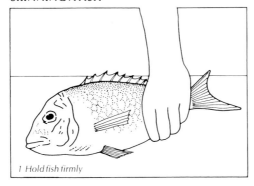

1 Hold fish firmly

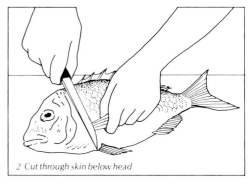

2 Cut through skin below head

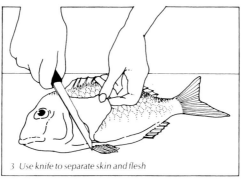

3 Use knife to separate skin and flesh

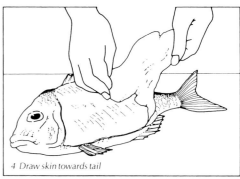

4 Draw skin towards tail

One of the major attractions of fish is the prospect of bringing home appetising fish of freshness markets and shops cannot match. The table quality of various species varies, of course, but most competent anglers have the chance to catch fish of first-class table quality. Space does not allow us to present any of the savoury recipes for our crayfish, shellfish and highly edible species, but we can help by providing basic instruction on how to get your catch to the pan in the best possible condition.

Cleaning, skinning and filleting is part of a successful fishing outing, the climax to catching a good meal. Start by laying the fish on its side and cutting in front and behind the gills with a sharp knife. Then slit the fish down the belly to the vent and cut under the gills to remove the entrails. Wash well in clean water, rubbing away any black lining. If the fish is to be stored treat it liberally with salt.

SKINNING:

Salt your fingers to prevent the fish slipping and then lay the fish on a flat surface. Make an incision around the neck and remove the pectoral fin. Slide the knife between the skin and the flesh separating them slightly. Then grasp the skin firmly in your fingers and pull the skin, severing it at the tail and repeating on the other side. With flatfish such as flounder or sole, make an incision at the tail and draw the skin quickly and firmly towards the head.

FILLETING A FISH

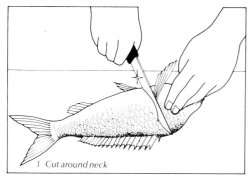

1 Cut around neck

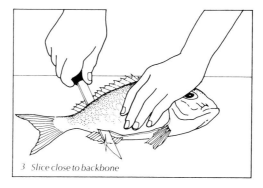

3 Slice close to backbone

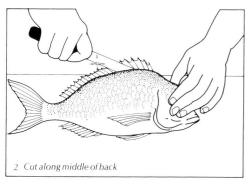

2 Cut along middle of back

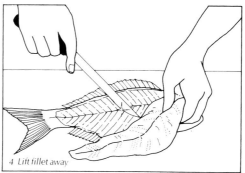

4 Lift fillet away

FILLETING THE CATCH:

Lay the clean fish on a flat surface, and with a sharp filleting knife cut it down the bone around the neck and along the middle of the back. Starting at the neck, slice the upper side of the fish cleanly from the backbone, keeping the knife as close as possible to the bone. Turn the fish over and repeat the process on the other side, removing small bones along the side separately. All fishermen enjoy bringing their catch home but there is nothing to equal the flavour of freshly caught fish barbecued on a river bank or in the outdoors.